HE SAID FOLLOW ME

BY.

DR. MARC A. GARCIA

EDITION 2

PUBLISHED BY:

ISBN 978-0-9884703-2-3

5 0 8 9 5>

9 780988 470323

TITLES OF CONTENTS

Dedication

To my Lord and Savior Yehshua who saw and sees what I am made of even when I had no idea.

To my son, Ricky, who is a leader in his own right; it is an honor to be called your father. Let Him who said Follow me be your trainer, leader, and mentor. He is calling you today – Follow Me!

And to my wife, Blanca Veronica Garcia whom after 10 years of marriage (as of May 2010) has shown me that behind every man of faith there is a powerful intercessor and prophet in his spouse who keeps him grounded.

To these 3 I say, thank you for believing in me and allowing me to be the man of Yahweh I am today. It is each of your characters that have molded me to be a father, husband, preacher, and Apostle.

I love you!

Dr. Marc A. Garcia

To the Reader:

This book is written with Hebrew wisdom because it is derived from the Living Word of God. The following should be considered by the reader before reading this book in its entirety. Without consideration of the following it may be possible that the reader will not be able to fully grasp the entire concept of this book.

The use of Yahweh and Yeshua are used because of the context of the Hebrew wisdom in this book; Yahweh referring to God (Hebrew) and Yeshua referring to Jesus and his Aramaic name. This is in no way a method for us to retract back to old testament ways and the way of old but to fully get in the "spirit" of this book I chose to use these names.

The words "Follow me" are not a casual invitation – it is an invitation given, to not only the disciples or the 12, but to each of us – you and I.

Bible Interpretation 101:

In Bible interpretation – there a 3 keys which must be taken into account as we study the Word of Yahweh and seek the depth of the wisdom in His word.

The three things consist of the following:

1. Context (the other 2 are subordinate to this one)
    a. Context is defined as the parts of a written or spoken statement that precede or follow a specific word or passage, usually influencing its meaning or effect.

b. Context takes into account the Who that is speaking; the Who that is being spoken to; and what the intent is of the person speaking.

2. Interpretation:

    a. Interpretation must be consistent in what is being read without removing the context.

3. Traditions:

    a. Traditions must be taken into view when looking at the Word. What traditions were in place? For example, is there anything behind Yehshua wearing a tunic?

The intent of this book is not to bring about a legalistic approach but to reveal truths to the reader by which are in the Word of Yahweh.

It is focused toward leaders in all stages, those who are active those yet to be but especially to those who have been wounded. My earnest prayer as you read, that your eyes be opened and that you hear the voice the Spirit of Yahweh revealing truth to your heart.

Chapter   1
The Foundation: Celebrations

Every major event in our lives is usually marked with a celebration. A birthday, a wedding, holidays. The thought pattern behind these celebrations is as vital as it is to live.

Each celebration is a reminder that a particular event occurred helping to shape you to be who you are.

After the wedding, your anniversary is celebrated to mark a new year of marriage. A celebration in today's society that is growing rarer year after year.

After your birth, a celebration occurs to mark the start of a new year of birth in this world. It denotes certain stages in one's life by which can be either a rite of passage or simply a little more freedom and responsibility.

Celebration is not a strange thing to God (who I will refer to as Yahweh His true name). It is certainly not strange to Jesus (who I will refer to as Yehshua).

Yahweh, after creating creation, He sat back and reviewed what He had done and said "It is very good". Genesis 1:31 says: *And God saw everything that he had made, and behold, it was very good.* It is interesting that the writer uses a superlative word there – "very". The Hebrew text for that word is: "meh-ode'" (spelled phonetically) which means much-ness, force, abundance, exceedingly. Then the word "good" is the Hebrew word "tobe" which means pleasant, agreeable, rich, valuable in estimation.

Now this was said after he formed the male and female (v.27) which means that this "very good" thing(s) created included you and me! He sat back and "celebrated" you and me in Adam and Eve.

Whether you believe it or not Yahweh delights in His creation. His creation may do some things which are not in His plan; however I believe Yahweh delights in His creation. If there is no evidence for you then I suggest you read John. For He so loved (fond of, loved dearly) the world that He gave His begotten son, that whosoever believeth in Him should not perish, but have everlasting life. Yahweh delights in His children.

One of the words to describe a celebration in the Old Testament is feast. There were numerous feasts, which marked a particular event, where the children of Yahweh where remembering what occurred that day. The Hebrew word for feast is "mishteh" – which means banquet. It is used 43 times in the Old Testament.

Then there is the Hebrew word "shabbathown" which means feast as well, but these where solemn feasts, used only 10 times in the Old Testament; 7 times in Leviticus.

Each of these words denotes that the nature of Yahweh is to celebrate and to allow His children to celebrate with Him.

When Yehshua was born there was a celebration. A rather private celebration but there was one. If we read into history and when His birth occurred you will find that the Maggai where not 3 people who came, it was a caravan of people; and history according to Josephus shows that they gave so much that it supported Yehshua's public ministry financially. We never see Yehshua taking an offering.

Yehshua while walking on this earth is no different. If celebrations where wrong for believers to attend then His example in going to the wedding is not a very good one;

after all the miracle at this celebration marked the beginning of His ministry as we know it.

It was a wedding at Cana. (Now there is so much symbolism in that alone but that is another book in itself). This wedding was where his stout follower and believer was with Him – His mother Mary. I find it most interesting that a wedding was used to give birth to a "ministry" that would culminate in a wedding. As we continue in that story in John 2 – Passover was upon them (v.13) yet again another celebration that we see Yehshua partaking in.

Now we must further understand that Yehshua walked the earth as a Jew. He was not a Greek, and contrary to what I may want to believe He was not Puerto Rican (my heritage). So there are many celebrations, patterns, rituals, and even "clichés" used by Yehshua which those to whom He was speaking to understand. You see I can give you a story concerning Puerto Rican folk lore, however unless you are Puerto Rican or have some good knowledge of the history you probably will not understand. That is why in today's society as much as people want to, they can never feel the hurt of racism felt by minorities, when they are not a minority.

Now we do not look to these rituals or celebrations and want to do them simply because Yehshua celebrated them; we look at them through the eyes of wanting to get to know more about our Savior who is our model for life, our pattern, not imitation. We are not called to imitate, we are called to let Him live through us and allow Him to manifest in our lives His character, not traditions.

Mathew 5:17 says;

Think not that I am come to destroy the law, or the prophets: I am not come to destroy, but to fulfill.

Yehshua said these words. The Law was designed so that nobody could accomplish it. It was like this from the beginning. It is designed so that we can see the need for a Savior. Someone to rescue us from the requirement of living under the law and rudiments once placed on a disobedient nation to bring order in their lives.

Yehshua lived and walked on this earth under that law, and He had to fulfill that Law, and thereby had to assure that He abided within that law because that would be the ONLY way He could fulfill it. You cannot fulfill a requirement by breaking it or destroying it, in that very act you have disqualified yourself.

In Matthew chapter 8 we see when Yehshua healed a leper, He told him go to the High Priest as it is required for his cleansing. This was law so He not only fulfilled it but enforced it (Leviticus 14:3 is the requirement). Mark 1:44 and Luke 5:14 offers the same recount of what Yehshua said to the man healed of leprosy.

Chapter   2
The Transition: From Boy to Manhood

Because Yehshua was raised in a Hebrew or Aramaic environment with a devout mother AND father there was one celebration which took place which the King James Bible has no recount by name, however we will see that it did happen.

It is the celebration of the Bar-Mitzvah. This celebration was/is established as a rite of passage for a young boy to enter into the ranks of manhood.

The Talmud refers to it many of times. Yet our Bible does not mention it however there are occasions which it does occur but it is not mentioned by name.

Genesis 21:8 (approx. 2066B.C)

And the child grew, and was weaned: and Abraham made a great feast the same day that Isaac was weaned.

Now the Hebrew word for grew is the word *"gaw-dal"* which means to grow in body, mind and honor. The word weaned is often interpreted as when the child is removed from the breast of its mother. However this is not the case here; the word weaned here is Hebrew for *"gaw-mal"* which means ripen, reached an age of maturity where he is held responsible for his actions and the parents are no longer held responsible before the eyes of Yahweh for his wrong doings.[1]

Samuel's weaning:

1 Samuel 1:15-28;

And Hannah answered and said, No, my lord, I am a woman of a sorrowful spirit: I have drunk neither wine nor strong drink, but have poured out my soul before the LORD. Count not thine handmaid for a daughter of Belial: for out of the abundance of my complaint and grief have I spoken hitherto. Then Eli answered and said, Go in peace: and the God of Israel grant thee thy petition that thou hast asked of him. And she said, Let thine handmaid find grace in thy sight. So the woman went her way, and did eat, and her countenance was no more sad. And they rose up in the morning early, and worshipped before the LORD, and returned, and came to their house to Ramah: and Elkanah knew Hannah his wife; and the LORD remembered her. Wherefore it came to pass, when the time was come about after Hannah had conceived , that she bare a son, and called his name Samuel, saying, Because I have asked him of the LORD. And the man Elkanah, and all his house, went up to offer unto the LORD the yearly sacrifice, and his vow. But Hannah went not up; for she said unto her husband, I will not go up until the child be weaned, and then I will bring him, that he may appear before the LORD, and there abide for ever. And Elkanah her husband said unto her, Do what seemeth thee good; tarry until thou have weaned him; only the LORD establish his word. So the woman abode, and gave her son suck until she weaned him. And when she had weaned him, she took him up with her, with three bullocks, and one ephah of flour, and a bottle of wine, and brought him unto the house of the LORD in Shiloh: and the child was young. And they slew a bullock, and brought the child to Eli. And she said, Oh my lord, as thy soul liveth, my lord, I am the woman that stood by thee here, praying unto the LORD. For this child I prayed; and the LORD hath given me my petition which I asked of him: Therefore also I have lent him to the LORD; as long as

*he liveth he shall be lent to the LORD. And he worshipped the
LORD there.*

Now if weaning really referred to the time when the child is
off the mother's breast then Hannah would be considered
an irresponsible mother. After she weaned him she would
hand him over to Eli forever. The average child is pulled
from the breast of the mother at the age of 2. Why would
she leave Samuel at the age of 2 to anyone?

The word wean is defined as to accustom a child to feed on
other than its mother's milk. According to the Talmud
Sopherim 18:11 after being trained (weaned) the mature
boy was brought before the priest to learn the law and obey
it.

1 Samuel 2:18-21

*But Samuel ministered before the LORD, being a child, girded
with a linen ephod. Moreover his mother made him a little
coat, and brought it to him from year to year, when she
came up with her husband to offer the yearly sacrifice. And
Eli blessed Elkanah and his wife, and said, The LORD give
thee seed of this woman for the loan which is lent to the
LORD. And they went unto their own home. And the LORD
visited Hannah, so that she conceived, and bare three sons
and two daughters. And the child Samuel grew before the
LORD.*

The word child there is not as we know it to be a child. This
word is the word Na'ar which means youth, servant; used 52
times in 1 Samuel alone including chapter 1 verse 22
mentioned above.

As mentioned earlier, according to the Talmud the young
boy will be presented to the priest. Josephus in his writings
shares this: *"When I was a child about fourteen years old, I
was commended by all for the love I had for learning, on*

which account the high priest and principal men of the city came to me in order to know my opinion regarding the accurate understanding of points of the Law"[2]

The Bar-Mitzvah for the Jewish people of today holds high regard. It marks the time when the young boy is now considered part of the men and is challenged to recite a particular blessing from the Torah. Not only that but he is counted as one of the men in temple when it comes time to open the Scriptures and read. Now, this may not seem important to us in today's day and age, however it is extremely important to the Jewish people. In Temple the Torah will not be opened and read unless there are 10 men present. That young boy has now been given the honor to be considered one of the men in qualifying if the WORD OF YAHWEH was to be read that day or not; a huge honor and privilege for that young man.

Now you may wonder – this is all Old Testament how do I apply this to the New Testament? First it is important to understand that ¼ of the New Testament are recounts and statements of people who were still living under the Law. All of the Gospels from which we get the basis for much of our faith were written in that time. Do not discount the Old Testament because the New is a "better covenant".

What many do not comprehend is that there are two separate laws which are referred to. One is the Law of Moses which contains those requirements for the "church of Moses" and then there is the Law or Ten Commandments. These Ten Commandments have not been removed, and it is not impossible to satisfy them. The Law of God and the Law of Moses are two very different things which we must make note of.

It is because of this reason we must be careful to read the Word of Yah in its context. The Law which Yehshua refers to is God's Law – He has come to fulfill that law. The Law of Moses was defined for the children of Israel to maintain a level of order. It is beyond the scope of this book however, where did Yehshua satisfy the Mosaic law which was the definition of religion? He came to fulfill the 10 commandments which is all about relationship. The Mosaic law is what He referred to when He spoke to the religious leaders in saying it is with your man made laws and doctrines which you have invalidated the Word or made it of null affect.

Look at Mathew 15; there is the clear depiction of this. The leaders ask Yehshua, "Why do thy disciples transgress the tradition of the elders? for they wash not their hands when they eat bread" (v2). Look at Yehshua's response: "Why do ye also transgress the commandment of God by your tradition? For God commanded , saying , Honour thy father and mother… (v3-4) His response is the Law of God referencing the 5th commandment. The Greek word used in verse 3 for commandment of God is "entole" - that which is prescribed to one by reason of his office; a commandment. Now, the word for commandments in verse 10 when He says, "commandments of men" is "entalma" which has more of a connotation of just a precept. A "precept" is a procedural directive or rule, as for the performance of some operation. He was saying that this had nothing to do with your procedures and has everything to do with the Law he had come to fulfill.

In essence what He said was that the Law of Moses was for Moses and the people. This was not for you to continue, but you folks went ahead and did it anyway.

Now you may think, "Dr. Marc you have just destroyed the primary point of your book". On the contrary – understand I am speaking and giving this example in the view that

Yehshua was a child under his "natural" parents' instruction. He had to adhere to the rules and traditions which He was a part of. However as you can see from his entire ministry He broke every one of those and found the opportunity to meet people where they were in their traditions.

Now in Hebrews 8:10 this is said:

For this is the covenant that I will make with the house of Israel after those days, saith the Lord; I will put my laws (Nomos=law) into their mind, and write them in their hearts: and I will be to them a God, and they shall be to me a people:

You see, the Law of Yahweh through your acceptance of Yehshua as your Savior is now written in your heart. You are the Israel of God which He has written this to. Yahweh was not speaking about the Law of Moses, with Jeremiah (Jeremiah 31:33) He was speaking about His Law (Hebrew word used is Towrah); because His Law is ALL based on relationship and that is His primary focus - relationship with His creation.

Here are some scriptures: Luke 24:44 says:

And he said unto them, These are the words which I spake unto you, while I was yet with you, that all things must be fulfilled , which were written in the law of Moses, and in the prophets, and in the psalms, concerning me.

Most people read this and think that the Law of Moses must have been fulfilled in Yehshua, no read it again it says, "*that all things must be fulfilled , which were written in the law of Moses, and in the prophets, and in the psalms, concerning me.*"

What was **written** in the Law of Moses concerning Him had to be fulfilled NOT the rudiments of the Law of Moses. Look at Yehshua's dealings with those who tried to get Him to walk in the Law of Moses.

John 7:19:

Did not Moses give you the law, and yet none of you keepeth the law? Why go ye about to kill me?

John 7:23

If a man on the sabbath day receive circumcision, that the law of Moses should not be broken ; are ye angry at me, because I have made a man every whit whole on the sabbath day?

Acts 13:39 says the following:

And by him all that believe are justified from all things, from which ye could not be justified by the Law of Moses.

This is what Paul refers to when he says that it is a "better covenant". The Law of Moses could not justify anyone, because it was meant to be a level of order and not to justify anybody. So that had to be nullified by the "First Law" to now establish a way of life. He brings it full circle.

It is for this very reason which the Pharisees asked, *"what is the greatest commandment?"* (Mathew 22) What was Yehshua's reply? That we must bring turtledoves as an offering? That we must offer the lamb or goat as a sacrifice? No – His response was clear and concise – (verses 37-40) *"Thou shalt love the Lord thy God with all thy heart, and with all thy soul, and with all thy mind. This is the first and great commandment. And the second is like unto it, Thou shalt love thy neighbor as thyself. On these two commandments hang all the law and the prophets."*

Look at the last part of His reply – *"On these two commandments hang ALL THE LAW and the PROPHETS".* You see the Mosaic Law or Law of Moses was undergirded by the

Ten Commandments but was established for the government of the church to have order.

Then as He said "Love the Lord thy God (elohyim) with all thy heart, mind and soul." The only way this can be done is if this law can be written in our mind and hearts. It all lies within itself.

For example, adultery is not a question of morality, it is really a question of love. If someone loves another they will not do something to hurt them. I believe the majority of all moral and social issues are a question of love and nothing more.

Chapter 3
The New Testament Bar-Mitzvah

Let's look at someone else other than Yehshua for a moment; the Apostle Paul. According to scripture he was circumcised on the 8th day, as he continues to share his spiritual "resume" he shares in Philippians 3 verse 5; "...as touching the law a Pharisee". In 1 Corinthians 13:11 Paul lets the church at Corinth know that there was a line of demarcation of maturity for him. It says:

When I was a child, I spake as a child, I understood as a child, I thought as a child: but when I became a man, I put away childish things.

The word 'became' is the Greek word "*gino-mal*" which means to be fulfilled. He became or celebrated a bar-mitzvah. He put away those childish – immature things. In its context it has nothing to do with baby things, but a maturity, a coming to a certain level of maturity. This is why he continues to say, "What I have known I know in part but as I mature I put myself in the position to learn more."

As mentioned before the celebrations and rituals had to be fulfilled by Yehshua so that He could fulfill the law in its entirety. Let us take a look to see where and how this happened.

First the bar-mitzvah had now become not only a celebration or rite of passage but became a "qualifier for the elite".

What would occur is that when the young boy presented himself at the age of 12 going on 13 he would present himself to the priest. The priest/rabbi will perform what is called a rabbinical interview. This interview consisted of the rabbi asking the young boy to essentially prove how well his parents had taught him the Torah. Also it was to prove whether he was worthy of continuing in the studies of the Torah and become a rabbi or not. We saw it earlier with the statement of Josephus.

Let's start with Mary, Joseph and Yehshua as a family.

Luke 2: 21-24: (cross reference Leviticus 12)

And when eight days were accomplished for the circumcising of the child *, his name was called JESUS, which was so named of the angel before he was conceived in the womb. And when the days of her purification according to the law of Moses were accomplished, they brought him to Jerusalem, to present him to the Lord;   (As it is written in the law of the Lord *, Every male that openeth the womb shall be called holy to the Lord;) And to offer a sacrifice according to that which is said in the law of the Lord, A pair of turtledoves, or two young pigeons.

Mary and Joseph had to adhere to the Law of Moses so that Yehshua would be "equipped" to fulfill the law.

The story continues in Luke 2:40-43:

And the child grew, and waxed strong in spirit, filled with wisdom: and the grace of God was upon him. Now his parents went to Jerusalem every year at the feast of the Passover. And when he was twelve years old, they went up to Jerusalem after the custom of the feast.

The feast of Passover was an every year occasion for this family. They went to celebrate the Passover which was the reminder of what Yahweh did amidst the children of Israel in getting them out of Egypt. Why, because it was part of the Mosaic Law.

Exodus 12:24 says,
And ye shall observe this thing for an ordinance to thee and to thy sons for ever.

Number 9:4 says,
Moses spake unto the children of Israel, that they should keep the Passover.

However something else occurred during this time. It says in verse 43 of Luke 2 – and when he was 12 years old they went up to Jerusalem after the custom of the feast. (Sound familiar?). He had to fulfill it – it was part of the requirements and his custom as a Jew. The history continues to go in a direction which seems to be unexpected. Mary and Joseph forget Yehshua in Jerusalem. Now we have to understand that this celebration of Passover was not small, families would gather together and make the trip together to celebrate the Passover. So it was not just Joseph, Mary, and Yehshua on a white donkey – it was a group of people who went with them. It is with this fact that we can now understand how they could travel and forget Yehshua. They just thought, "it's ok he is probably with a cousin or one of his brothers". But when they figured out that they left him they turned back.

Now I never lost my son anywhere but my wife has for a brief stint. Can you imagine what went through their minds; these were the two who had been entrusted with Yehshua? So many prophetic words were spoken of Him. In fact earlier in Luke 2 we see some of them being uttered (Luke 2:25-40). When they frantically get to the temple after 3 days of searching, they find Yehshua sitting there speaking with the "doctors and scribes" (in other words the elite priests and rabbis) they gasp for air and run to him. These "elites" were astonished by this young boy/man's understanding of scriptures. This is essentially Yehshua's rabbinical interview. Now I believe He would have passed that interview and someone would want to mentor him to be a rabbi. Most recounts do not share what happened there; but all recount the conversation that occurred between Him and his natural parents.

Verses 48b-50 shares:

Son, why hast thou thus dealt with us? behold , thy father and I have sought thee sorrowing . And he said unto them, How is it that ye sought me? wist ye not that I must be about my Father's business? And they understood not the saying which he spake unto them.

It is interesting to note that his mother, Mary was the one who was confronting him with the fact that they were searching for Him. His reply causes some confusion in His parents. He (paraphrased by me) says, Why where you looking for me don't you know I am about my Father's business.

Chapter 4
My Father's Business?

His parents look at Him perplexed at what He just said, because they were looking at that statement through their natural eyes. They were asking within themselves – you are not making a table. Your father is a carpenter – what are you talking about? Yehshua was telling them He was doing THE Father's business.

Now this may seem elementary revelation – however there is so much more in there. The word for Father there is Pater. Now the important fact we need to understand is that during the rabbinical interview the young boy is asked questions. The group of rabbis will then make a decision if he is worthy of being mentored by a rabbi to become a rabbi.

If the young boy fails the interview the rabbi will simply tell him "You have failed and you should go about your father's business." This is when the father takes the helm and begins to show the young man "his trade" so that the young man will have an inheritance and trade.

So Yehshua was "completing" or answering his own rabbinical interview. He did not allow the "elite" to decide.

It is worth noting that the priesthood mentioned in the New Testament had become this from the Old Testament lineage process – where the priesthood was reserved for a "select" family.

That being said, we know that each of the 12 disciples where of Jewish decent. So that would mean that they lived under the law and therefore the customs of every other Jewish boy. (Understand that the Bat-Mitzvah, the same celebration but without the qualification process for girls, was not established until the early 1800's – the term boy is not meant as a bias). Each of the Apostles had to undergo the same process. They had a bar-mitzvah and thereby had a rabbinical interview. Yet what happened? None of them were rabbis; this would indicate that each of them failed the interview and where told by the rabbi, "Go be about your father's business". Each of them was working a trade.

What happens following is amazing to say the least. After being in the desert for 40 days and nights, Yehshua comes back walking on the coast of Galilee (Mathew 4:18) and finds himself two men Simon and Andrew. He finds them casting a net as they are fisherman. Furthermore He says to them the most powerful words that can be said to these two men – "Follow me (v.19)." Why is it so powerful? The reason is because the word "follow" is the Greek word "deute" which means (literally translated) come hither, come here, come. For most of us this means nothing. However coming from a Rabbi at that time it meant everything. As this is exactly what the Rabbi would say to a young boy/man who was undergoing his rabbinical interview and the Rabbi wanted to be his mentor. It was a calling into discipleship or mentoring of a Rabbi.

1 Kings 19 shows us the calling of Elisha. As unorthodox as it can be- this is the example of unorthodox. Elijah comes up to Elisha while he was working and takes his mantle and throws it on Elisha and keeps walking. Elisha goes after him and says, "Let me say goodbye to my people then I will go with you." (Paraphrased) Elisha KNEW what that meant. Elisha KNEW that these events where for him to leave all and follow after this man who "appeared" out of nowhere.

Look at what Elijah replies to him, "Go back then – what have I done to you?" (v.20 paraphrased)

These two brothers, Simon and Andrew, whom Yehshua called, were rejected by the "elite". However this Rabbi who just came out of the wilderness now appears to them and tells them essentially – let me mentor you! They who have rejected you missed it – I see your full potential because my Father is the one who predestined you for it.

This entire scenario repeats itself for each of the disciples.

Chapter 5
Follow me – I believe in you!

The elite did not believe in the 12, blessed Yahweh He believes in you because He knows what He has deposited into you.

What attracted the disciples was not that Yehshua offered them a huge salary, on the contrary, when He confronted a rich young man it made all of them think, "what am I here for?"

Look at the level of belief He had in each of them. Luke 6:13 says:

And when it was day, he called unto him his disciples: and of them he chose twelve, whom also he named apostles;

First and foremost I want to take a moment and explain what an Apostle is but first let me share what it is NOT. It is not a "rank", a level of leadership, a title to be used lightly. It is however a level of leadership, a rank within the Body of Yehshua by function not to feed into the egos of men. By definition used in the above scripture Apostle (apostolos) is as a delegate, messenger, one sent forth with orders. One sent forth with "orders"; I love that definition, because it denotes a position of leadership but also subordination. He does not give himself orders but the one who is above him gives him the orders.

Hebrews 3:1 says, Yehshua is our Apostle and High Priest of our profession. Yet He calls these 12 something that has not been uttered yet in all of scriptures – Apostles.

What does this mean? It means two things:

1. He saw the potential in them to be who and what they were called to be and had been dormant for some time.
2. He made them plural and equal by function to Himself.

He named (onomazo – to utter) them Apostles, those who were rejected by society, those who had no ministerial experience other than the very short period of time with Yehshua. This was also way before the mandate to go forth. Did he make them to be the messiah as well – NO! He put them by function (sent one) on the same plane as himself.

John 17:18 says;

*"As thou hast **sent** me into the world, even so have I also **sent** them into the world."*

Romans 10:15 says;

*"and how shall the preach, except they be **sent**"*

Isaiah in his 52nd chapter speaking of Yehshua says exactly what is quoted there in verse 7.

Yahweh uses the simple to confound (cause confusion) the wise. You see everyone thought that they were "so wise" in doing what they were doing and selecting people based on their qualifications and what they had to offer, but Yahweh is not impressed with natural fleshly qualifications.

You see when society tells you, you are not worthy for the priesthood or any other calling you know Yahweh has called you to, it does not matter. Yehshua is the One who calls and He is saying "Follow me!"

88% of Christians do not have any answer to the question – What is your calling? Most use the scripture where Yehshua sent them out, to evangelize and yet that is everyone's mandate. However there is so much more to do on His behalf.

Yehshua named them apostles before the mandate He gave them to go out and make disciples found in Mathew 28. Let's take a look, verses 16-20 says:

"Then the eleven disciples went away into Galilee, into a mountain where Jesus had appointed them. And when they saw him, they worshipped him: but some doubted. And Jesus came and spake unto them, saying, All power is given unto me in heaven and in earth. Go ye therefore, and teach all nations, baptizing them in the name of the Father, and of the Son, and of the Holy Ghost: Teaching them to observe all things whatsoever I have commanded you: and, lo , I am with you always, even unto the end of the world."

This scripture, contrary to popular belief, has nothing to do with evangelism, and has everything to do with discipleship. Their mandate by Yehshua at this point was to go and make Apostles. Go make and produce after your own kind – "sent one's". Teaching them whatsoever He (Yehshua) had commanded them to do.

Now what happens to so many people is that once the person who helped them realize their potential is gone (for whatever reason), then they do not "feel" called anymore. They go back to what they were doing. The Apostles are not exempt of this either. After Yehshua being crucified and not yet being resurrected each of them went their own way.

John 21 is the picture of so many in the Body of Yehshua who have aborted what Yahweh has called them to do. They heard the voice of Yehshua tell them – "Follow Me". But for whatever reason they have allowed themselves to fall back into what is comfortable to them.

You see the call of Yahweh in your life will stay dormant until you decide to enter into it. You can live a life in most standards as "successful" but I believe when the scripture says, what is it worth to gain the whole world and lose your soul, has very little to do with salvation but more to do with what He has called you to do. You lose your soul when you lose your identity, your purpose.

You see just like in John 21, you can try to run from your calling however what you run to will seem like a laborious task, with no fruit. No we are not talking about fruit in money, money is not fruit it is a by-product of a service rendered. The fruit I speak of is your spiritual growth, the spiritual growth of your family. These are fruit.

Today as you read this I want you to give you John 21 in today's language if I may. I am not taking or adding into this at all and not declaring doctrine out of it, but it is an attempt to make it practical to you:

Verses 2-6

There were together Marc Garcia, and John called Mathews, and Jerry of Albuquerque, and the sons of Mr. Rockefeller, and two other of his followers. Marc Garcia saith unto them, I am going back to work as a pharmacist. They say unto him, John, yeah I am going back to my law practice. Jerry says unto them I am going back to my cleaning business. They all went forth, and entered into their perspective locations; and that year their family struggled. Marc always being away left his son to fend for himself and now is living a lascivious lifestyle. John due to his law practice his wife wants nothing more to do with him. Jerry finds himself alone as everyone has left him but when the new year has now come, Jesus stood on their shore(s): but they knew not that it was Jesus. Then Jesus saith unto them, Children, have ye any fruit? They answered him, No. And he said to each of them, try again now, and ye shall find. They each tried again, and now they were able to be restored to the point where they could not contain their joy.

Now I want you to put your name in there and your current occupation (keep in mind it may very well be that where you are is in fact your calling – this is for folks who know there is something else they should be doing).

You spent a year trying and nothing suddenly Yehshua appears. Your friends around you say – "Look it is Yehshua!" You, like Simon, get on your coat and jump in to get to Him. Why? Because you remember the first time he visited you and where you were and nobody believed in you, nobody could see your potential, but He did the moment He saw you and said "Follow me!"

Today as you read this book – Yehshua is standing on the shore of where you are and is calling you once again! "Come! COME with me! Let me continue to mentor you. Our relationship has not ended because you think I am not around anymore. It has just started!"

You may say, I have to wait until this is done, until this is taken care of. Yehshua calls you, not necessarily when it is convenient, but when it is His timing, because the calling requires faith to stand amidst the challenges.

John 4:34 says:

Jesus saith unto them, My meat is to do the will of him that sent me, and to finish his work.

He was telling them – my sustenance, my food is to do the will of Him who sent me and to FINISH His work. You are called to be a part of the FINSHED work. It is up to you to discover the details of that call so that you can move in it and grow and have fruit.

Your true satisfaction in life is reached when you find out what you are supposed to be doing, and do it until completion.

Perhaps there has been some event in your life as traumatic as the disciples seeing their Lord crucified. I have had my own painful experiences with my leadership, yet I know what I have been called to do. Has there been temptation to give up and close shop? YES! I say YES vehemently, but greater is the call than the circumstances that present themselves to hinder the same.

Chapter 6
YOU CAN DO IT!

When traumatic events occur in our lives we have two choices; allow the emotion to control our future decisions or allow the experience to mold our leadership. The latter is not the most popular choice, but that does not change the fact that it is the right one.

When something occurs with the leadership we are working with, it feels like such a deep hurt. The Apostles felt that hurt when Yehshua was crucified. It shook their entire foundation; their dreams; their aspirations. They more than likely blamed Judas for the entire thing, not fully understanding it was Yahweh's plan to have this occur.

Most (not all) betrayal or traumatic events are allowed by Yahweh to form and fashion us into His image. Not everything that happens is the devil. For example when you go outside in the cold without a coat and get a cold – it was not the devil it was you. Don't rebuke the devil, if you want to spend energy rebuking someone, rebuke yourself.

One KEY thing to all of this is that we must understand that these events are not a "surprise" for Yahweh. He knew it was going to happen, and as for me I have learned that if we review after the fact – there where indicators to let me know what was going to happen.

If someone would have told me what I would've gone through, I probably would not have entered into what He has called me to.

I like to use the phrase "Yahweh is setting you up". This phrase denotes so much of what I have learned. You see hardships and betrayal are a part of life in this world. If anyone tells you that walking out your calling will be easy it is a lie. However it can pleasurable even in the midst of the challenges. Let me share.

The eyes of faith are the eyes or view of Yahweh. Your eyes cannot perceive or imagine what He has set for you. Neither has eye seen or ear heard…. This is a truth for every believer but for leaders primarily. For I know the plans I have for you says the Lord (Jeremiah 29:11). He was speaking to Jeremiah as a leader.

If HE knows the plans He has for us, than our key focus in everything that we do must be to get to know Him, because in Him are the details of the plan. He is the architect and we are the hired contractors.

Arise into the words that He is speaking into your spirit right now – Follow me! Forget that others did not believe in you. Forget that others have treated you unfairly. FOLLOW ME! Not them.

Yahweh has you as part of His plan. His plan will be completed but He so wants to use you. I am bold enough to tell you as you read this book – Yehshua is calling you forth; calling you out of the rejection, out of the mediocrity, out of survival mentality into a supernatural move in your life.

Remember the Apostles went through the "selection" process and were pushed away to follow the trade their father was doing, until the Rabbi of rabbi's appeared and said to each of them as He is saying to you right now – "Follow me". Let go of your past rejections; let go of your past hurts, learn from them take those lessons with you but "Follow me". Follow Him to where He wants to take you. I guarantee that it is so much more than what you can imagine or think.

Closing:

Brother/Sister in the Lord, my sole desire is that you refocus, recommit to what He has called you to do. If you are not sure what He has called you to do, then spend serious time in fellowship with Him and He will tell you. Always remember the final "decider" is you. Only you can obey what He tells you – nobody else.

As mentioned His plan will come to fruition but HE SO LONGS to have you as a part of it. The question is, "Are you willing?" He will not force you or twist your arm, it is that willing and yielded vessel He will use to manifest His Glory on this earth. You are a wonderful candidate enjoy the journey!

Reference Page:

The following is a short list of reference material used that can be reviewed for validity and understanding:

Chapter 2 reference:

(1) http://www.jewishencyclopedia.com/view.jsp?artid=239&letter=B&search=Bar%20Mitzvah

(2)   http://www.ccel.org/j/josephus/works/autobiog.htm

Dr. Marc Garcia – Biography:

Dr. Marc Garcia is a prolific teacher/preacher of the Word of God. With his attention to detail of the Word, he focuses on really getting into the context of the Word before sharing it as a spiritual truth or doctrine.

Dr. Garcia has authored many articles on the subject of leadership, the Christian Walk, and the prophetic. He is amazing in mending his theological doctorate degree with a spirit filled teaching to really grasp the understanding of the Word of God.

Dr Garcia has worked in the secular realm with 15 years of IT experience as well as before coming to the Lord a record producer for artists in the rap industry in NY. These talents equipped him to be the principle recording engineer for the church's first contemporary worship CD recording; Es Bien Grande.

In June of 2008 he received his doctorate in Biblical Studies/Theology from North Carolina College of Theology, Wilmington, NC.

With the understanding that he and his wife Blanca are called to be Apostles to "burnt stones", they do not take this calling lightly.

As of September 2009 he and Prophet Blanca have been ordained as CIAN ministers under the apostleship of Apostles Jerry and Martha Hester of Dominion Community Church. This has renewed Dr. Garcia's vision to raise and equip leaders into their destiny.

Dr. Garcia is president of Radio-Mar, a music only Christian radio station playing contemporary Latin Christian music. Dr Garcia has launched "Empresarios Para Dios" to help the growing Latino community in implementing biblical principles into their businesses. He and his wife are preparing to launch their school Triangle Institute for Ministry Excellence and online college to help the saints become who God has declared they are..

Dr Garcia has traveled to Rwanda in focus of the call to raise leaders. He has also traveled to Peru on a missions trip and ministered to pastors and leaders as well. He does have plans to travel to Rwanda again in 2010 as well as Kenya to activate the people of Africa in their prophetic destiny.

www.ingramcontent.com/pod-product-compliance
Lightning Source LLC
Chambersburg PA
CBHW071802020426
42331CB00008B/2369